Selectively Sourced

We recall, in the not so distant past, a time when 'Organic' was what we grew in our gardens or bought at the local produce stand. There were no 'non-GMO' products because genetically modifying our food sources was science fiction and not yet science fact.

Welcome to Shipetaukin®, where we have chosen to carry and support only the best, most natural and wholesome products. We know that consumers are becoming more choosy about the foods they put in and on their bodies, so we have selected some of the best to carry our brand and to showcase on our site.

Come visit us at www.Shipetaukin.com.

Sign up at our site to receive notification when our upcoming titles are published:

- Cooking with Gluten Free Fonio Recipes, Vol. 2
- Baking with Gluten Free Fonio
- Superfruit Smoothies Featuring Moringa Leaf Powder and Baobab Powder

Acknowledgements:

Kevin Beck - Editing

Mariana Piaz – Recipes, photography, and editing

K Deutsch – Cover photo, recipes, photography, and photo editing

Kathryn Roberts – Photo editing, stylistic elements

Alexandra McClure – Layout editing

K.G. Kehoe – Concept

Contents

About Fonio:

Fonio is one of the most ancient of grains. It is the smallest member of the millet family, native to West Africa where it flourishes in poor soil and variable weather conditions. The tiny seeds are nutrition powerhouses. Fonio is rich in protein, offering 12 grams per cup, as well as essential amino acids including methionine and cystine. With a low glycemic index and plenty of fiber, fonio is an ideal choice for diabetics as well as those concerned with avoiding blood sugar spikes. Its especially high iron and folic acid content make it a great food choice for all women, especially those who are pregnant. This amazing little grain is known in African lore as the Seed of the Universe. It is easy to digest and therefore of benefit to those with sensitive stomachs, and especially the elderly.

Vegan and naturally gluten free, fonio easily adapts to recipes which call for quinoa or rice. Where rice is bland and quinoa is somewhat muddy or earthy in taste, fonio digitalis (white fonio) has a light nutty flavor that nicely complements vegetables and fruits. Toasting the grain before cooking enhances this flavor profile and helps prevent the small grains from becoming mushy when cooked in liquid. Finely ground fonio becomes a versatile all-purpose gluten free flour, which can be used in baking, as well as to add layers of taste, texture, and nutrition to any recipe.

Shipetaukin® Fonio comes in three forms: raw, couscous, and milled flour. While the fonio couscous version is convenient, American cooks are partial to experimenting with the raw product in the same way they use other grains. Being able to build a recipe from the bottom up and cook the fonio according to specification is key to layering flavor and texture. *All recipes in this cookbook begin with raw Shipetaukin Fonio,* which is clean and ready to use straight out of the bag – no rinsing is required. Some incorporate Shipetaukin Fonio Flour, both for baking and coating. Feel free to substitute our couscous version, or to cook your fonio and freeze ahead of time to speed up meal prep.

We also offer Boabab Super Fruit Powder and Moringa Leaf Powder which are powerhouse foods on their own. Our deliciously complex dark amber African Honey is quite unique and makes clover honey pale in comparison. Look for upcoming cookbooks featuring more of these unique and wholesome flavors of Africa.

Come visit us at www.Shipetaukin.com, where you will find gathered in one place many natural and wholesome products for your entire family – including your pets – plus our own wonderful brand.

Basic Prepared Fonio:

Toasting fonio brings out its nutty flavor and helps the tiny seeds absorb liquid to become soft without disintegrating. This form is used in many of our recipes. Make extra to set aside for meals throughout the week. Raw Shipetaukin Fonio is clean and ready to be used straight out of the bag – *no rinsing is required* – unlike some other brands.

Use 1 cup raw fonio to 1 $^1/_3$ cups liquid.

In a dry cast iron or non-stick pan: Over medium heat, stir raw fonio continuously for several minutes until it begins to brown. Slowly add the liquid, a bit at a time, while continuing to stir. Do not add the liquid all at once, rather allow it to become incorporated before adding more. This will take 4 to 5 minutes. Remove from heat, cover, and let stand 10 minutes. Fluff with a fork.

Fonio Cereal:

Use 1 part Shipetaukin raw fonio to 6 parts liquid (water, milk, or milk substitute). Bring liquid to a boil, then reduce heat to low and slowly add the fonio while stirring constantly. When the fonio is nice and creamy, transfer to bowls and drizzle with honey, maple syrup or agave if sweetness is desired. Top with berries for extra fiber, and nuts which complement the natural flavor of fonio while adding texture and nutrition.

For our recipes:

We recommend wherever possible that you use organic, fair trade, and/or locally sourced food. Food in its most natural state is always best for our bodies.

The recipes here are all gluten free and feature the wonderful and tasty fonio grain from Africa. Make them your own by adapting them to your dietary needs. Simple substitutions and adjustments will make them vegetarian (lentils instead of chicken) or vegan (nutritional yeast instead of cheese), for example.

We love Shipetaukin fonio, and we hope this introduction to our new favorite versatile pantry staple will make you a fonio lover too!

Fruity Fonio Cereal

Here's a tasty twist on fonio's most basic use as a hot cereal. Try milk instead of water for an even creamier treat.

Ingredients:

6 cups - water
½ cup - coconut milk
1 cup - fonio, raw
1 cup - mixed berries
4 tbsp - Shipetaukin African Honey

1. Bring liquids to a boil.
2. Add fonio and gently stir until it has a creamy consistency.
3. Add the mixed berries blend until smooth.
4. Top with honey and serve.

Serves 4

| Calories 311 | Sugars 20.5 g | Carbohydrate 71.7 g |
| Fat 1.5 g | Protein 3.5 g | Dietary Fiber 2.1 g |

Breakfast Scramble

Fill up your day with this high-quality protein recipe. We suggest using organic, cage-free eggs.

Ingredients:

3 eggs
1 tbsp - olive oil
½ cups - cherry tomatoes, halved
⅛ cup - diced white onion
¼ cup - fresh mozzarella pearls
¼ cup - fonio, basic prepared

Salt and pepper to taste.

1. Beat the eggs in a bowl, then add the fonio and halved tomatoes.
2. Heat the oil in a skillet over medium heat, then add the egg mixture, regularly folding until the eggs are nearly set.
3. Stir in mozzarella pearls and continue folding the mixture. As the cheese gets to its melting point, remove from heat and serve.

Serves 2

| Calories 225 | Sugars 3.4 g | Carbohydrate 22.2 g |
| Fat 24.8 g | Protein 30.6 g | Dietary Fiber 1.6 g |

Lemon Protein Yogurt

Where healthy and delicious meet. We suggest using Greek yogurt to increase protein intake.

Ingredients:

½ cup - fonio, basic prepared
1 cup - lemon custard yogurt
½ cup - applesauce
2 tbsp - chia seeds

Dried cranberries to taste

Sprinkle nuts as desired
(chopped pecans and peanuts
used here)

1. Mix all other ingredients with the prepared fonio.
2. Serve with a slice of melon for a sweet finish.

Serves 2

| Calories 270 | Sugars 18.9 g | Carbohydrate 46.1 g |
| Fat 5.9 g | Protein 7.6 g | Dietary Fiber 6.0 g |

Berry Breakfast

Keep some prepared fonio on hand to throw together this quick morning treat.

Ingredients:

1 cup - fonio, basic prepared
½ cup - pecans, chopped
½ cup - walnuts, chopped
½ cup - almonds, slivered
½ cup - dried cranberries
½ cup - strawberries, chopped
½ cup - pure maple syrup

1. In a serving bowl, mix the strawberries, cranberries, and nuts.
2. Add the fonio and maple syrup, stirring thoroughly.
3. Serve immediately, either on its own or with pancakes, waffles, or French toast.

Serves 4

| Calories 490 | Sugars 36.1 g | Carbohydrate 63.1 g |
| Fat 27.2 g | Protein 7.3 g | Dietary Fiber 5.5 g |

Overnight Fonio

The best way to start your day is to stay out of the kitchen and have everything ready when you are.

Ingredients:

⅓ cup - fonio, raw
⅓ cup - almond milk
1 tsp - Shipetaukin African Honey
½ cup - plain Greek yogurt
½ cup - berries (or fruit of your choice)

1. Toast the fonio for 3-5 minutes in a dry pan over medium heat until golden brown.
2. In your choice of container, layer the ingredients. Start with the fonio, followed by almond milk, honey, yogurt, and finally the fruit. Refrigerate overnight.
3. Enjoy the next morning by either mixing it all together or eating it parfait style.

Serves 1

Calories 476	Sugars 26.4 g	Carbohydrate 95.2 g
Fat 2.2 g	Protein 17.8 g	Dietary Fiber 3.3 g

Cheesy Fritata

We suggest using organic free-range eggs for fabulously fresh flavor. Don't be afraid to add your favorite fillings and seasonally fresh veggies.

Ingredients:

5 large eggs
1 cup - milk
½ cup - fonio, toasted
¼ cup - fonio, toasted (reserved)
¼ cup - green onions, diced
2 cloves garlic, minced
½ cup - cherub or grape tomatoes, quartered
½ cup - mushrooms, roughly chopped
1 cup - baby spinach, roughly chopped
½ cup - shredded mozzarella
2 tbsp - olive oil
1 tbsp - balsamic vinegar
1 tsp - salt
1 tsp - pepper

1. Preheat oven to 350°F
2. In a large bowl, beat the eggs and milk until smooth, then add salt and pepper.
3. In an oven proof skillet, sauté the ½ cup toasted fonio, spinach, mushrooms, and green onions on medium heat until the veggies have softened.
4. Turn off heat and incorporate the egg mixture with the sautéed vegetables.
5. Place the skillet in the oven and bake for 15-20 minutes, until set. In the meantime, mix the olive oil, vinegar, and chopped garlic until well-integrated. Soak the tomatoes in the mix until the frittata is done baking.
6. Remove from the oven, spread the balsamic-olive oil and tomato mixture on top along with mozzarella cheese and the reserved fonio.
7. Cut into quarters and serve.

Serves 4

Calories 355	Sugars 4.9 g	Carbohydrate 32.8 g
Fat 17.5 g	Protein 15.7 g	Dietary Fiber 0.9 g

Fonio Coated Shrimp

Savor this classic dish. You can use any size shrimp though coating larger shrimp is usually easier.

Ingredients:

¼ cup - water
1 egg, beaten
1 cup - fonio flour
24 shrimp
2 tbsp - coconut oil
1 tsp - red pepper flakes

1. Dredge shrimp with fonio flour, then with the beaten egg, and once again with the fonio flour.
2. Heat oil over medium-high heat in a large skillet and cook shrimp on each side until golden brown.
3. Serve warm with red pepper flakes and drizzled Sriracha sauce.

Serves 4

| Calories 241 | Sugars 0.0 g | Carbohydrate 38.4 g |
| Fat 4.6 g | Protein 11.5 g | Dietary Fiber 1.1 g |

Bacalao a la Vizcaina

This dish is packed with antioxidants and is a great source of fiber.

Ingredients:

2 lbs salted cod
4 potatoes, sliced thick
2 large onions, sliced thick
2 tsp - capers
2 large cloves garlic, minced
¼ cup - pitted green olives
4 oz jar - roasted red bell peppers, drained and chopped
1 bay leaf
8 oz can - tomato sauce
½ cup - extra virgin olive oil
1 cup - water
¼ cup - white wine
2 eggs
1 cup - fonio flour

1. Soak the salted cod in about 2 quarts of water, changing the water 3 times over the course of 8 hours. Drain and cut the fish into bite-size pieces.
2. Coat the cod with egg then dredge in the flour.
3. Layer half of each ingredient in a stock pot in the following order: potatoes, cod, onions, capers, garlic, olives, and roasted red peppers. Place the bay leaf on top, then pour half the tomato sauce and half the olive oil. Repeat with the remaining ingredients in the same order. Pour the water and white wine on top. Do not stir.
4. Cover and bring to a boil over medium heat. Reduce heat to medium-low and simmer until the potatoes are tender, about 30 minutes, then serve.

Serves 4

| Calories 927 | Sugars 8.9 g | Carbohydrate 86.7 g |
| Fat 35.5 g | Protein 62.6 g | Dietary Fiber 9.2 g |

BBQ Meatballs

This recipe is a great entree for family dinner, or as party appetizers. Enjoy the sweet flavor of the BBQ sauce mixed with the nuttiness of the fonio.

Ingredients:

2 lbs ground beef
1 cup - fonio flour
¼ cup - chopped onion
½ cup - milk
1½ tsp - salt
2 eggs

BBQ Sauce:

1 cup - organic ketchup
½ cup - Shipetaukin African Honey
¼ cup - white vinegar
¼ cup - molasses
1 tsp - liquid smoke flavoring
½ tsp - salt
½ tsp - ground black pepper
¼ tsp - paprika
¼ tsp - chili powder
¼ tsp - onion powder
¼ tsp - garlic powder
¼ tsp - cayenne pepper

1. Preheat oven to 375°
2. Stir ketchup, honey, vinegar, and molasses together in a saucepan over medium heat until smooth; add liquid smoke, salt, black pepper, paprika, chili powder, onion powder, garlic powder, and cayenne. Stir the seasonings into the ketchup mixture, reduce heat to low, and simmer until thickened, about 20 minutes. This yields approximately 1½ cups.
3. In a large bowl, combine the beef, fonio flour, onion, milk, salt and eggs. Shape into small meatballs, about 1 inch in diameter and place on a baking sheet.
4. Bake for 25 to 30 minutes, then combine with sauce and serve.

Serves 4

| Calories 580 | Sugars 42.7 g | Carbohydrate 70.0 g |
| Fat 23.9 g | Protein 20.5 g | Dietary Fiber 1.6 g |

Chicken Tikka Masala

A savory Indian dish that has a tomato-based sauce and traditional spice blends. Pairing with cooked fonio instead of rice adds balance and nutrition.

Sauce:

1 tbsp - ginger, grated
¾ cup - tomato sauce
1 cup - coconut cream
1 tbsp - butter, melted
1 tbsp - cornstarch
1 tbsp - lemon juice
1 tbsp - garam masala
½ tsp - cumin
½ tsp - paprika
½ tsp - turmeric
½ tsp - cayenne pepper
1 tbsp - fonio, toasted
1 bay leaf
½ onion, diced
2 garlic cloves, minced

Ingredients:

1 lb - chicken breast, cubed
2 cups - fonio, basic prepared

1. In a bowl, mix together all ingredients for the sauce and set aside.
2. Add the chicken to a crockpot, cover with sauce, and stir to evenly distribute.
3. Cook 6-8 hours on low (or 3-4 hours on high).
4. Serve with prepared fonio.

Serves 4

Calories 541
Fat 25.0 g

Sugars 3.4 g
Protein 31.0 g

Carbohydrate 46.3 g
Dietary Fiber 2.9 g

Hearty Jambalaya

This simple recipe incorporates both Spanish and French influences and makes a delicious winter stew.

Ingredients:

1 cup - fonio, raw
1½ cups - chicken bone broth
½ cup - water
3 tbsp - fonio, toasted
2½ tbsp - Cajun seasoning
2 tbsp - olive oil
14 oz can - tomato sauce
1 purple onion, diced
½ green pepper, diced
2 cloves garlic, minced
1 large turkey sausage link
1 cup - raw shrimp

Salt and pepper to taste

1. Combine all ingredients except shrimp in a large skillet and bring to a boil, then allow mix to simmer for about 30 minutes, stirring frequently.
2. Add shrimp for the last 4-5 minutes.
3. Serve.

Alternatively, you can add everything to a crockpot and let it cook on high for 1 hour or low for 2 hours, adding shrimp in the last 5 minutes.

Serves 4

| Calories 614 | Sugars 7.0 g | Carbohydrate 46.8 g |
| Fat 22.2 g | Protein 56.6 g | Dietary Fiber 3.1 g |

Grammy's Gnocchi

Try this filling meal with your choice of sauce or grass fed butter.

Ingredients:

2 potatoes
2 cups - fonio flour
1 egg

1. Bring a large pot of salted water to a boil. Peel potatoes and add to pot. Cook until tender but still firm, about 15 minutes. Drain, cool and mash with a fork or potato masher.
2. Combine 1 cup mashed potato, flour and egg in a large bowl. Knead until dough forms a ball. Shape small portions of the dough into long rods on a floured surface. Cut the cylinders into half-inch pieces.
3. Bring a large pot of lightly salted water to a boil. Drop gnocchi carefully and cook for 3 to 5 minutes or until gnocchi have risen to the top; drain in a colander and serve.

Serves 4

| Calories 432 | Sugars 0.9 g | Carbohydrate 92.9 g |
| Fat 2.8 g | Protein 9.4 g | Dietary Fiber 4.6 g |

Mexican Fonio

Easy to prepare and can be included in any Mexican dish. Try it in your favorite taco or burrito.

Ingredients:

6 tbsp - olive oil
1 cup - white rice, uncooked
1 cup - fonio, raw
2 tsp - minced garlic
1 tsp - salt
1 tsp - cumin
1 cup - tomato sauce
28 oz chicken bone broth
⅓ cup - cilantro, diced

1. Heat olive oil in a large pan over medium heat.
2. Add the fonio and rice and stir until it begins to brown.
3. Mix in the garlic, salt, and cumin and stir until golden.
4. Stir in the tomato sauce and chicken broth and turn the heat up to medium-high.
5. Bring to a boil, then turn the heat to low and cover pan with lid.
6. Simmer on low for 20 to 25 minutes.
7. Remove from heat and fluff with a fork, then stir in chopped cilantro and serve.

Serves 4

Calories 488	Sugars 3.0 g	Carbohydrate 67.5 g
Fat 22.6 g	Protein 6.0 g	Dietary Fiber 1.9 g

Texmex Bowl

After making "Mexican Fonio", set extra aside for a quick and easy weekday supper like this crowd pleasing bowl.

Ingredients:

2 cups - warmed or room temperature 'Mexican Fonio' from page 15.
8 oz - black beans
Fresh corn from 1 ear (about 8 ounces)
2 large beefsteak tomatoes, diced
2 large avocados, diced
1 cup - Mexican blend cheese, shredded

1. Drain and rinse the black beans.
2. In a bowl, mix the Mexican Fonio, black beans, corn, diced tomatoes, and avocado.
3. Sprinkle cheese on top and serve with Fonio Tortilla Chips from page 33.

Serves 4

| Calories 488 (Needs Cals) | Sugars 3.0 g | Carbohydrate 67.5 g |
| Fat 22.6 g | Protein 6.0 g | Dietary Fiber 1.9 g |

Gluten Free Pasta

Enjoy this recipe of classic noodles.

Ingredients:

4 cups - gluten free flour
2 cups - fonio flour
4 eggs

Salt
Olive oil

1 cup - water (for adding to
    dough as needed)

1. On a clean surface, scoop out the mixed flour into a mound on the work surface.
2. Make a well in the flour.
3. Crack eggs into the well and mix carefully with a fork or your fingers (pay close attention that the walls of the well don't collapse so that your egg mixture can be properly integrated into the flour).
4. Begin to knead when the eggs and flour start to form a dough-like consistency.
5. Knead until the dough is springy to the touch (add water if dough becomes dry or cakey).
6. Cover dough and let it rest for 30 minutes.
7. Spread more flour on your work surface and roll the dough until it is thin and translucent.
8. Cut the dough into desired shape (ribbon shapes if you would like to make noodles or squares and circles for stuffed pasta).
9. Bring 2 quarts of water to a boil and season with salt and olive oil.
10. Cook pasta for 5 minutes, or until al dente, and prepare as desired.

Serves 6

| Calories 281 | Sugars 0.1 g | Carbohydrate 51.0 g |
| Fat 4.95 g | Protein 8.2 g | Dietary Fiber 1.3 g |

Ravioli

Serve this Italian-style filled pasta as is, or add marinara sauce and vegetables to create a casserole.

Ingredients:

½ cup - fonio flour
2 eggs
½ cup - ricotta
8 oz - baby spinach
3 cloves garlic, minced
1 cup - mushrooms, sautéed
½ onion, diced and sautéed
1 tbsp - olive oil

For the dough: see Gluten Free Pasta recipe on page 17.

1. Mix fonio flour, ricotta, spinach, and eggs together in a bowl.
2. In a pan, sauté mushrooms with butter and garlic. Cook until soft then allow to cool.
3. Add mushrooms into the filling and mix well.
4. Put mixture into a piping bag or a plastic bag with a corner snipped.
5. Spread some flour onto clean work surface and roll out dough until thin and translucent.
6. Splitting the dough into 2 sections, pipe filling onto dough as dollops, leaving ¾ - 1 inch of space on every side.
7. Brush water between every dollop to make a grid, and place the second section of dough on top, lightly pressing down to seal the dough around the filling.
8. Cut with a pizza cutter or a sharp knife between every ravioli and separate. If necessary, crimp each side of the raviolis with a fork to ensure the pasta is well sealed.
9. Bring 2 quarts of water to boil with salt and olive oil to taste. Cook the pasta for 5 minutes or until al dente and serve as desired.

Serves 6

Calories 806
Fat 11.5 g

Sugars 1.0 g
Protein 21.4 g

Carbohydrate 152.2 g
Dietary Fiber 5.4

Spinach Mushroom Marsala

A recipie packed with tons of flavor thanks to the Marsala, garlic, and tomatoes. It's the perfect meatless meal to serve over nutty fonio.

Ingredients:

1 tbsp - olive oil
2 bags - baby spinach, 10 oz ea.
2 large sweet onions, chopped
6 oz mushrooms, sliced
2 cups - fonio, basic prepared
6 ounces Marsala

Salt and pepper to taste

1. Add the onions to a lightly oiled wok or skillet, stirring often over medium heat until golden.
2. Add mushrooms, stirring until the mushrooms have started to soften.
3. Season with salt and pepper.
4. Add Marsala.
5. Continue stirring until wine is mostly evaporated.
6. Add spinach, mixing well.
7. Cook just until the spinach wilts.
8. Serve over prepared fonio.

Serves 2

| Calories 627 | Sugars 8.9 g | Carbohydrate 100.9 g |
| Fat 8.3 g | Protein 15.4 g | Dietary Fiber 11.4 g |

Sweet Pepper Bowl

Our healthy and guilt-free recipe is packed with tons of flavor.

Ingredients:

1 bell pepper, diced
2 cups - jasmine rice, raw
1 cup - fonio, raw
4 cups - water
1 cup - lime juice
2 tbsp - cilantro, diced
1 tbsp - minced garlic
2 tbsp - olive oil
Dash of sea salt

Sauce:

8 tbsp - olive oil
8 tbsp - lemon juice
1 tbsp - cayenne
½ cup - fresh cilantro

Serves 4

1. Cook rice and fonio with the water and the lime juice in a rice cooker.
2. Fluff the fonio and rice, and in a bowl combine with the garlic, olive oil and salt. Let it sit for several minutes, then add the cilantro and stir again.
3. Serve with sauce.

Calories 673	Sugars 1.9 g	Carbohydrate 85.7 g
Fat 34.9 g	Protein 6.2 g	Dietary Fiber 1.9 g

Smoked Gouda
Mac & Cheese

Make it veggie-riffic by adding butternut squash, cauliflower, or roasted Brussels sprouts.

Ingredients:

1 lb - gluten free elbow pasta
½ cup + 2 tbsp - grass fed butter
½ cup - fonio flour
4 cups - coconut milk
6 cups - freshly shredded smoked gouda
½ tsp - kosher or sea salt
½ tsp - pepper
1 cup - fonio, raw

1. Prepare pasta according to package directions.
2. Melt ½ cup butter in large saucepan over medium heat. Sprinkle in fonio flour and whisk and cook 2-3 minutes. Add salt and pepper.
3. Slowly pour in milk, whisking until smooth and heating to a low boil until thickened. Do not stop whisking and cooking until thick. Remove from heat.
4. Grease a 9"x13" baking dish and add the hot pasta to the dish. Sprinkle the cheese over the top.
5. Pour thickened cream sauce over hot pasta and cheese, letting it sit until the cheese melts. Stir everything together.
6. Melt 2 tbsp butter over medium heat in a skillet. Add in the fonio, stirring constantly for 3-5 minutes or until golden brown.
7. Sprinkle fonio over the mac and cheese.
8. Bake in a preheated 325º oven for 12-15 minutes, then serve.

Serves 6

Calories 850	Sugars 5.1 g	Carbohydrate 109.1 g
Fat 36.1 g	Protein 26.8 g	Dietary Fiber 2.2 g

Vegetable Stir Fry

An easy recipe that's big on flavor and packed with anti-oxidants.

Ingredients:

4 cups - broccoli florets
2 cups - cauliflower florets
¼ cup - water
3 tbsp - fonio, toasted
2 tbsp - olive oil
1 tbsp - Shipetaukin African Honey
3 tbsp - onion, diced
1 tbsp - garlic clove, minced
4 tbsp - soy sauce
2 tbsp - lemon juice
4 cups - fonio, basic prepared

Sliced almonds or peanuts (as desired)
Salt and pepper to taste

1. Heat oil in pan over medium-high heat.
2. Add broccoli, cauliflower, water, and toasted fonio to pan. Stir together for a few minutes to heat the veggies.
3. Add honey, onion, garlic, soy sauce, and lemon juice.
4. Toss until the ingredients are thoroughly mixed together and the vegetables are tender.
5. Serve over basic prepared fonio.

Serves 4

| Calories 493 | Sugars 8.4 g | Carbohydrate 95.7 g |
| Fat 8.8 g | Protein 10.7 g | Dietary Fiber 8.3 g |

Mediterranean Salad

This crisp, savory salad makes a great accompaniment to any main dish.

Ingredients:

1 cup - fonio, basic prepared
1 medium cucumber, diced
8 oz - grape tomatoes, halved
1 red bell pepper, diced
1 cup - fresh parsley, minced
1 small red onion, diced
1 cup - Kalamata olives, halved
4 oz - crumbled feta

Dressing:

¼ cup - olive oil
¼ cup - red wine vinegar
½ tsp - dried oregano
½ tsp - pepper
½ tsp - salt
1 tbsp - fresh dill
1 tsp - Shipetaukin African Honey
1 tsp - lemon juice

1. Place fonio, cucumber, tomatoes, onions, pepper, parsley, olives, and feta in a large mixing bowl and toss.
2. Combine dressing ingredients in a small bowl.
3. Pour the dressing over the salad, toss to combine, and set aside for at least 30 minutes to allow the flavors to develop.

Serves 2

| Calories 255 | Sugars 2.8 g | Carbohydrate 3.9 g |
| Fat 28.1 g | Protein 0.2 g | Dietary Fiber 0.3 g |

Stuffed Zucchini Boats

These treats are the perfect midday snack at only 127 calories.

Ingredients:

2 zucchini, cut lengthwise
1 cup - fonio, basic prepared
2 tbsp - olive oil
2 tbsp - balsamic vinegar
¼ cup - red onions, diced
3 cloves garlic, minced
2 cups - baby spinach,
coarsely chopped
1 cup - mushrooms, chopped
1 cup - shredded mozzarella
¼ tsp - red pepper flakes

Salt and pepper to taste

1. Position a rack in the center of the oven and preheat the oven to 400º. Spray a baking dish with cooking spray. Using a measuring spoon or melon baller, scoop out the center of the zucchini leaving a ¼ inch border on all sides. Chop and reserve the zucchini pulp. Place the zucchini in the prepared baking dish, skin side down and set aside.
2. Heat the olive oil in a skillet over medium high heat. Add the onions and mushrooms and cook for 3-4 minutes or until they start to soften, then add the zucchini pulp, pepper flakes and garlic, and cook until the zucchini softens. Add the baby spinach and fonio, stirring to thoroughly combine. Season.
3. Divide the mixture into the prepared zucchini. Top with cheese, cover with foil and bake for 30-35 minutes. Remove the foil during the last 2 minutes of baking and set the oven to broil until the cheese is bubbly. Cut each in half crosswise and serve.

Makes 8 Boats

| Calories 127 | Sugars 1.7 g | Carbohydrate 13.3 g |
| Fat 5.8 g | Protein 5.6 g | Dietary Fiber 1.6 g |

Garden Side Salad

Where healthy and colorful meet.

Dressing:

2 small garlic cloves
½ tsp - Himalayan salt
1 tbsp - Shipetaukin African Honey
¼ cup + 2 tbsp - olive oil
¼ cup + 2 tbsp - water

Ingredients:

16 oz - fresh baby spinach
1 head - romaine lettuce
1 cup - fonio, basic prepared
½ cup - walnuts, chopped
½ cup - almonds, slivered
½ cup - dried cranberries
½ cup - strawberries, chopped

For the Dressing:

1. Combine all of the ingredients in a blender, and process until completely smooth and emulsified.
2. Chill for 4 hours to allow the flavors to develop. Shake well before serving.

For the Salad:

1. Chop romaine lettuce into ½ inch pieces and toss with cleaned and dried baby spinach.
2. Put lettuce and spinach on a large platter and top with the chopped nuts, strawberries, cranberries, and cooked fonio.
3. Toss with the prepared dressing and serve.

Serves 4

Calories 551	Sugars 16.2 g	Carbohydrate 51.0 g
Fat 37.1 g	Protein 10.5 g	Dietary Fiber 10.0 g

Grilled Vegetable Salad

Grilled vegetables become succulent and sweet, and pair beautifully with fonio.

Ingredients:

4 cups - fonio, basic prepared
1 zucchini, sliced lengthwise into ½"
thick planks
1 yellow squash, sliced lengthwise
into ½" think planks
1 red bell pepper, halved & seeded
1 yellow bell pepper, halved &
seeded
1 large sweet onion, skin on, halved
⅓ cup - extra virgin olive oil
½ tsp - freshly ground black pepper
½ tsp - salt
3 tbsp - red wine vinegar
2 tbsp - Dijon mustard
½ cup - fresh basil, chopped

1. Brush vegetables on all sides with 4 tsp olive oil, and season with salt and pepper.
2. Grill over medium heat, turning after 3 minutes, until the vegetables soften and start to char a bit. Remove to a large bowl, cover loosely, and allow the vegetables to steam as they cool.
3. While the vegetables rest, whisk together the vinegar and mustard. Slowly whisk in the remaining olive oil.
4. Discarding the onion skin, chop the vegetables and return to the same bowl, retaining any juices. Add the cooked fonio, salt and pepper, and toss. Drizzle the vinaigrette over the bowl and stir to combine. Mix in chopped basil just before serving.

Note: You can serve this salad chilled or at room temperature. Preparing the day before allows the flavors to develop. Add basil just before serving to keep its flavor and texture bright.

Serves 8

| Calories 307 | Sugars 2.6 g | Carbohydrate 42.0 g |
| Fat 12.8 g | Protein 6.6 g | Dietary Fiber 2.5 g |

Tomato Salad

Super simple, fresh, and bursting with antioxidants.

Ingredients:

2½ cups - cherry tomatoes, halved
if large
¼ cup - fonio, toasted
½ cup - fonio, basic prepared
½ cup - fresh mozzarella pearls
3 tbsp - basil, chopped
2 tbsp - almonds

Dressing:

⅓ cup - balsamic vinegar
¼ cup - organic virgin olive oil
¼ cup - water
2 tbsp - oregano
½ tsp - garlic, chopped
1 tsp - Dijon mustard

1. Mix all the dressing ingredients together
   and set aside.
2. In a large bowl, toss together the
   tomatoes, fonio, mozzarella, basil and
   almonds.
3. Pour the dressing over the salad and mix
   to combine.

Serves 5

| Calories 230 | Sugars 12.0 g | Carbohydrate 30.4 g |
| Fat 10.9 g | Protein 3.3 g | Dietary Fiber 4.9 g |

Very Berry

Try this refreshing treat that incorporates the health benefit of fonio with the sweetness and juicy flavors of berries.

Ingredients:

2 cups - fonio, basic prepared
1 ½ cups - strawberries, cut in half
1 cup - raspberries
1 cup - blackberries
1 cup - blueberries
1 tbsp - finely chopped mint
1 tbsp - finely chopped basil

Citrus Honey Dressing:

1 tsp - orange zest
4 tbsp - fresh orange juice
1 tsp - fresh lemon juice
1 tbsp - fresh lime juice
1 tbsp - Shipetaukin African Honey
1 tsp - finely chopped mint
1 tsp - finely chopped basil

Serves 4

1. To prepare the dressing: in a small container, whisk together orange zest, orange juice, lemon juice, lime, juice, honey, mint, and basil. Set aside.
2. In a large bowl, combine prepared fonio, strawberries, raspberries, blueberries, mint and basil. Gently stir.
3. Drizzle citrus honey dressing over the salad and gently stir again.

Calories 240
Fat 1.1 g

Sugars 15.2 g
Protein 3.3 g

Carbohydrate 56.2 g
Dietary Fiber 6.9 g

Refreshing Citrusy Salad

Cool and light, this make-ahead salad pairs well with something from the grill.

Ingredients:

4 cups - fonio, basic prepared*
¼ cup - freshly squeezed lime juice
3 tbsp - extra virgin olive oil
1 cup - diced peeled and seeded cucumber
½ cup - diced pineapple
½ cup - diced mango
½ cup - thinly sliced red onion
½ cup - packed fresh cilantro, chopped
4 tbsp - coarsely chopped pistachios
¼ tsp - freshly ground black pepper

Salt to taste

1. Combine the specially prepared fonio, cucumber, onion and fruit in a large bowl.
2. Whisk together the olive oil and lime juice and drizzle over the salad, tossing to coat.
3. Stir in pistachios, pepper and cilantro.
4. Season with salt to taste.

*When preparing the fonio for the salad, instead of water use equal amounts of freshly squeezed orange juice and chicken or vegetable broth. This can be done ahead or the day before.

Serves 8

| Calories 235 | Sugars 4.4 g | Carbohydrate 39.2 g |
| Fat 7.5 g | Protein 3.1 g | Dietary Fiber 1.5 g |

Bell Pepper Quiche Minis

Using a combination of peppers adds color, flavor and nutrition. Try spicing things up with jalapenos!

Ingredients:

1 cup - mixed bell peppers, finely diced
¼ cup - onions, diced
⅓ cup - fonio, basic prepared
¼ cup - cilantro, chopped
1 uncooked gluten free pie crust
4 eggs
1 cup - milk
1 tsp - salt

Small muffin pan
Parchment paper

1. Preheat oven to 375F.
2. Use a cookie cutter or glass to cut small circles in the pie crust.
3. Line muffin tins with parchment paper, then stretch pie crusts into prepared tins.
4. Wisk the milk, eggs, and salt in a large bowl.
5. Combine the remaining ingredients in a bowl, then pour into egg mixture and stir to incorporate evenly. Ladle about 3-4 tablespoons of quiche mixture into each crust.
6. Cook for 20-25 minutes and serve warm.

Makes 12 Quiches, 2 per serving

| Calories 237 | Sugars 2.7 g | Carbohydrate 17.0 g |
| Fat 14.2 g | Protein 10.6 g | Dietary Fiber 1.0 g |

Peanut Butter Cups

A delicious and healthy alternative to regular sugar-packed peanut butter cup candies.

Ingredients

2 cups - sugar free chocolate chips
2 cups - peanuts
¼ cup - fonio, raw
1½ + ½ tbsp - coconut oil

mini cupcake liners
mini cupcake pan
piping bag

1. In a grinder or food processor, grind the peanuts, fonio, and 1½ tbsp coconut oil into a nut butter and set aside. Use additional oil to reach desired consistency.
2. Microwave chocolate chips with remaining coconut oil in 15 second increments until smooth.
3. Pour melted chocolate mix in a thin layer on the bottom of each liner.
4. Using a piping bag, carefully place the peanut butter on the chocolate leaving space on the sides. (Store excess fonio infused peanut butter in a fridge for use in other recipes.)
5. Add remaining chocolate to the tops and sides and let cool in fridge.

Makes 8 cups, 2 per serving

Calories 334	Sugars 20.6 g	Carbohydrate 30.6 g
Fat 25.2 g	Protein 3.4 g	Dietary Fiber 4.0 g

Peanut Butter Granola Bars

These healthy snacks are perfect as a quick treat and make a welcome addition to lunchboxes.

Ingredients:

1 ½ cup - fonio, raw
1 cup - steel cut oats
½ cup - pecans and peanuts mix, crushed
½ cup - 'fonio peanut butter' from page 31
½ cup - coconut oil (more as needed to achieve creamy consistency)

Parchment paper

1. Preheat oven to 375°.
2. Mix all dry ingredients together in one bowl.
3. Combine the oil and peanut butter in another bowl and warm in microwave for 20 seconds. Then stir to create a smooth mix.
4. Add wet ingredients to the dry ingredients, mixing thoroughly. Using your hands, pack and pat the granola into bars on a parchment paper lined cookie sheet.
5. Allow granola bars to cool or serve warm with sauteed bananas and drizzled chocolate.

Makes 8 Bars , 1 per serving

Calories 375
Fat 17.1 g

Sugars 0.7 g
Protein 8.3 g

Carbohydrate 50.5 g
Dietary Fiber 3.8 g

Fonio Tortillas

The traditional flavor of masa harina nicely complements the nuttiness of fonio for a unique twist on this meal time staple.

Ingredients:

2 cups - masa harina (corn flour or Maseca)
1 cup - fonio flour
Pinch of salt
3 tbsp - avacado oil

1. Combine the masa harina, fonio flour, salt, and water in a mixing bowl. Knead to form a smooth, moist dough with a playdough-like consistency. If the mixture is too dry or too wet, add more water or masa harina in teaspoon increments.

2. Working with 1 portion at a time, place dough between 2 sheets of plastic wrap on a tortilla press. Flatten dough, turn dough one-half turn and flatten again. Remove dough from the press, and then remove the plastic from dough.

3. Heat oil in skillet over medium heat. Cook 15 to 30 seconds or until tortilla releases itself from the skillet. Turn tortilla; cook 30 seconds or until brown spots form. Turn again; cook another 30 to 45 seconds or until it puffs like pita bread. Remove from pan. Keep warm. Repeat procedure with remaining dough.

*Note: To make Tortilla Chips, cut the tortillas into 4 or 6 equal pieces and fry them until crisp.

Serves 4

| Calories 307 | Sugars 0.0 g | Carbohydrate 53.3 g |
| Fat 8.8 g | Protein 6.0 g | Dietary Fiber 3.3 g |

Pupusas

A pupusa is a traditional Salvadoran dish of thick corn tortillas stuffed with a savory filling.

Ingredients:

Dough from "Fonio Tortillas" on page 33.
1 cup - grated cheese: quesillo, queso fresco, Monterey Jack, or mozzarella
3 tbsp - avacado oil

1. Combine the masa harina, fonio flour, salt, and water in a mixing bowl. Knead to form a smooth, moist dough with a playdough-like consistency. If the mixture is too dry, add more water, one teaspoon at a time. If the mixture is too sticky, add more masa harina, one teaspoon at a time.
2. Cover the bowl with a clean towel and let stand for 10 minutes. With lightly oiled hands, form the dough into 8 balls about 2 inches in diameter.
3. Using your thumb, make an indentation into one of the balls, forming a small cup. Fill the cup with 1 tablespoon of cheese and wrap the dough around the filling to seal it. Making sure that the filling does not leak, pat the dough between your hands to form a round disk about 1/4-inch thick. Repeat with the remaining balls.
4. Heat a lightly oiled skillet over medium-high heat. Cook the pupusas for 2 to 3 minutes on each side until golden brown. Serve warm.

Serves 4

| Calories 544 | Sugars 0.3 g | Carbohydrate 80.6 g |
| Fat 19.5 g | Protein 15.2 g | Dietary Fiber 5.0 g |

Coconut Pudding

This delicious treat is perfect for any snacking occasion. Keep them cooled and ready to go at a moment's notice.

Ingredients:

2 cups - coconut milk
½ cup - coconut cream
1 cup - fonio, raw
4 tbsp - Shipetaukin African Honey, plus more as needed
1 tbsp - brown sugar
½ tsp - salt
¼ tsp - vanilla or almond extract

Recommended toppings: chopped nuts, coconut flakes, dried cranberries or raisins, sliced bananas, or chocolate.

1. Place the milk, cream, fonio, honey, and salt in a medium saucepan and bring to a boil over medium-high heat.
2. Lower the heat to barely a simmer and cook uncovered, stirring occasionally, until the fonio is tender and the mixture thickens, roughly 20 minutes.
3. Remove from the heat and stir in the vanilla or almond extract. Taste, adding additional honey or toppings as desired.
4. Serve warm or chilled.

Serves 4

| Calories 152 | Sugars 26.1 g | Carbohydrate 27.9 g |
| Fat 4.0 g | Protein 4.1 g | Dietary Fiber 0.0 g |

Rosh Hashanah Apples

Rosh Hashanah is the Jewish New Year. It is typical to celebrate by eating apples as a way to wish one another a sweet new year.

Ingredients:

apples of choice, sliced
1 cup - Shipetaukin African Honey
¼ cup - Greek yogurt
½ cup - organic whipped cream cheese
½ cup - pecans
½ cup - almonds
¾ cup - fonio, raw
1 tsp - cinnamon
2 tsp - brown sugar

1. Blend pecans, almonds, Greek yogurt, fonio, and half of the honey in a blender until smooth.
2. Pour the mixture into a bowl and fold in the cream cheese until integrated, then whip the mixture with a whisk until it is smooth and thick.
3. Add in the rest of the honey as well as the cinnamon and brown sugar.
4. Serve immediately or store in fridge for up to a week.

Makes 24 Servings

Calories 110	Sugars 12.3 g	Carbohydrate 19.5 g
Fat 3.7 g	Protein 1.4 g	Dietary Fiber .09 g

Banana Cheesecake

These healthy snacks are delicious for any time of the day and satisfy that savory craving.

Crust Ingredients:

1 cup - fonio, basic prepared
¼ cup - brown sugar
4 tbsp - butter, melted

Filling Ingredients:

8 oz - organic cream cheese, softened
1 tbsp - Shipetaukin African Honey
1 banana, mashed
¼ tsp - vanilla extract
8 oz - dark chocolate, melted

1. Mix the brown sugar into the melted butter then with the fonio. If the mixture is too runny add more cooked fonio. Press into the bottom of a greased, 9x9 baking pan.
2. Bake at 350° for 10 minutes or until the edges begin to brown. Set aside for 10 minutes to cool.
3. Beat the cream cheese, honey, mashed banana, and vanilla until smooth and creamy, then pour over the cooled crust.
4. Allow the filling to set and then pour melted chocolate over the top and smooth it out with the bottom of a spoon.
5. Chill for one hour, cut into bars, and serve.

Makes 4-6 Bars

Calories 648   Sugars 49.5 g   Carbohydrate 75.6 g
Fat 42.8 g   Protein 3.8 g   Dietary Fiber 5.5 g

Chocolate Banana Mug

This microwave meal is a great healthy treat and is ready in minutes.

Ingredients:

½ cup - fonio, raw
¼ cup - almond milk
1 tbsp - Shipetaukin African Honey
1 banana, overly ripe
3 tbsp - hazelnut spread

1. Mix together fonio, milk, and honey in a mug and microwave on high for 2 minutes.
2. Stir in banana and hazelnut spread and heat for 2 minutes at 50% power, stirring every 30 seconds.

*Note: Microwaves vary; time and power may need to be adjusted for best results.

Serves 2

| Calories 467 | Sugars 33.2 g | Carbohydrate 89.4 g |
| Fat 9.5 g | Protein 6.9 g | Dietary Fiber 3.0 g |

Chocolate Cupcakes

This love-at-first-sight recipe is perfect for any occasion.

Ingredients:

2 cups - fonio, basic prepared
⅓ cup - milk
4 large eggs
1 tsp - pure vanilla extract
¾ cup - butter, melted and cooled
1½ cups - granulated sugar
1 cup - unsweetened cocoa powder
1½ tsp - baking powder
½ tsp - baking soda
½ tsp - salt

Frosting:

2¼ cups - heavy whipping cream
1¼ cups - semisweet or bittersweet chocolate chips

1. Preheat the oven to 350º. Grease a cupcake tray (or use cupcake liners).
2. Combine the milk, eggs and vanilla in a blender or food processor. Process just until combined. Add the cooked fonio and the butter. Blend well until smooth.
3. In a large bowl, mix the dry ingredients together. Add the contents from the blender and stir until combined.
4. Pour the batter into the cupcake tins and bake on a rack in the middle position for 25-30 minutes or until a toothpick inserted in the center comes out clean.
5. Cool the cakes completely on a cooling rack.
6. For the frosting, place the chocolate chips in a medium bowl. Heat the whipping cream in a saucepan until it gently simmers. Pour the hot cream over the chocolate chips and let the mixture sit for five minutes. Whisk to combine until it is smooth. Refrigerate 2-3 hours until completely chilled. Use an electric mixer to whip the frosting to soft peaks.
7. Spread onto the cupcakes and chill for at least 2 hours before serving to let the frosting set.

Serves 12

| Calories 278 | Sugars 25.6 g | Carbohydrate 37.8 g |
| Fat 14.3 g | Protein 4.3 g | Dietary Fiber 2.5 |

Made in the USA
Middletown, DE
10 September 2022

10188722R00024